FUN-TASTIC!

DENYS PARSONS

FUN-TASTIC!

Illustrated by
Cornelia Ziegler

A Piccolo Original

PAN BOOKS LTD
LONDON

First published 1971 by Pan Books Ltd,
33 Tothill Street, London, S.W.1

ISBN 0 330 02792 1

2nd Printing 1971
3rd Printing 1972

Printed in Great Britain by
Cox & Wyman Ltd, London, Reading and Fakenham

Introduction

Since I was at school I have been collecting misprints and mistakes which appear in newspapers and magazines. These have made me laugh so much that I have spent many hours wondering what causes them.

What makes the printer press the wrong keys? You all know about QWERTYUIOP on the top line of the typewriter. Well, the keys on the machines which set type for printing go like this: ETAOIN SHRDLU CMFWYP. I have a theory – and nobody has contested it – that a mischievous character, whom I have named Gobfrey Shrdlu, haunts newspaper offices and causes these printing errors, grammatical slips, and double meanings.

One of the best ways to enjoy these Shrdlu items is for one member of the family to read them aloud to the rest - if he can do so without choking or doubling up on the floor.

Whoever is responsible for this path would be doing a public duty by compelling the removal of the barbed wire. May this catch the eye of the authorities.

Letter in Devon paper

```
              NOTICE

F. J. Battick, CBM, has been appointed
to exterminate all mongoose on the
station, and has been authorized to
destroy any of these animals found
about the station using an air rifle.
```

US Naval Air-station order

Q. What does the name *Lear* mean in Shakespeare's *King Lear*?
A. It is of Celtic origin and means SLEEVE VALVE ENGINE.

Washington Daily News

Speed of drying of wood is primarily dependent upon the rate of removal of moisture from the timber.

The Guardian

Our picture shows Mr Robert Tenter rolling the lawn with his fiancée, Miss Elizabeth Briarcliffe.

Bucks paper

Gourmets will be interested in an instant coffee with egg, bottled garlic and preserved onion rings.

Chicago Sun-Times

To any youngster I say: 'Treat your boots as your friends and grease them twice a week'.

Daily Express

'I no longer know the meaning of indigestion,' writes Mr Godfrey Farnham, health expert. 'Nowadays I can eat a heavy meal while walking at top speed up a steep hill.'

Weekly paper

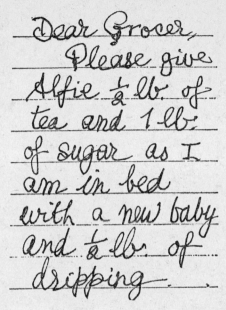

Dear Grocer,
Please give Alfie ½ lb. of tea and 1 lb. of sugar as I am in bed with a new baby and ½ lb. of dripping.

Letter received by grocer

He leaned his head against her hair. A wasp strayed across his face. He kissed it.

from a novel

Their marriage was solemnized before an arch decorated with large baskets of bride, officiated. She was attired roses decorated the base of the arch. The bride was given in marriage by her father, Rev Philip Guter, uncle of the point at her wrists. Her head, in a white lace gown with a fitted bolero and long fitted sleeves coming to a bride, served as bridesmaid.

Indiana paper

Mr and Mrs John Bowley are the parents of their child, a daughter born at Windsor hospital on August 15th.

Rutland (Vermont) paper

Not so long ago Brian's mother bowled to him in their garden at Yeadon; she is now in hospital.

Daily Express

Q. When does the Navy consider a man to be 38 years of age?

A. The Navy considers a man to be 38 on his 28th birthday.

Stockton (Calif.) *Record*

SEVENTEEN-YEAR OLD LOCUSTS
TO APPEAR NEXT SUMMER

State Collee, Pa. Dec. 11th – The 17 yearg lgocgugst is due to appear agaginngg gnext summer, according to G. H. Hadley, Jr, an entomolegeggggbmn TTMMggggobrr . . . jEas logist at the Pennsylvania State College.

Erie Daily Times

The match was unfinished owing to measles. Craghurst was compelled to scratch.

The Harrovian

In carrying his bath right through the innings on Thursday for 125, A.O. Jones has made a brilliant start.

Irish Field

The first three balls yielded four runs. Then the bowler took a very long swift run – and bit the off stump.

Yorkshire paper

'How can you say such a thing about him?' she gasped. 'I'm certain of one thing – whatever may come between us, and wherever he may be on this earth, Arthur will always remember that I love ham.'

Short story

Then add the milk and the butter and rub the mixture well into the floor.

Cookery book

☛ Due to copy error, we regret that the Surprise Apple Sweet Potato recipe in the October issue was incomplete. Please add: 4 cups of mashed potatoes and 3 large apples.

Cannery publication

> The restaurant is open from 12 noon till midnight. Worm meals will be served before the theatre.

Notice in Munich restaurant

The many friends of Mrs Barrett will be sorry to learn that she injured her foot on Sunday. It will probably be six weeks before the fool can be released from a plaster cast.

Canadian paper

Cigar connoisseur writes of Blank's cigars: 'Extremely good value at the price.' Prove it for yourself by sending 22s for a sample of six – you will give them to your friends.

Advert in South London paper

Today's hint tells you how to keep your hair in first-class order. Cut it out and paste it on a piece of cardboard and hang it in your bathroom.

Essex paper

SHEFFIELD MAN'S MACHINE STRUCK TELEPHONE POLE
Both in Hospital

Sheffield paper

We sent sixty dresses to Miss Forsythe in December, and we have just heard that she is using our gift in roofing the Mission House.

Report of Hibernian Church Missionary Society

For what lad can behold a pretty girl weeping for him without drying her ears on his breast.

Boston Globe

Our photograph shows Mr and Mrs H.J.Hill leaping the Hurlingham Church Hall yesterday after the marriage ceremony.

Buenos Aires Herald

Well-built modern house in 2 excellent self-contained flats. An opportunity not to be missed. Bath vacant in the early spring.

Gloucester Echo

She was sorry she had agreed to sleep in the haunted house, because all night long she was troubled by strange whiskers in her ear.

Serial story

Miss Sutton struck out in all directions, and the nurses called for help. However, when Dr Jackling arrived she had been overpowdered.

Short story

A HOSPITAL SPOKESMAN SAID
HIS CONDITION IS
'CATISFAMTORY'

News wire to *Chicago Daily News*

FOR SALE – Doctor's sailing dinghy and accessories. Doctor no further use.

Yorkshire paper

The route taken by the Queen was lined by clapping, cheering crows.

Leicester Evening Mail

The Roman Catholics obtained a firm footing in Central Africa, and sent forth several missionaries into the equatorial regions. They were accustomed to begin their work by buying heathen children and educating them. The easiest and best way to prepare them is first to wipe them with a clean towel; then place them in dripping-pans and bake them until they are tender. Then you will have no difficulty in rubbing them through a sieve, and will save time by not being obliged to cut them in slices and cook for several hours.

Montreal paper

At the end of the two-hour itinerary, refreshments were provided by Ready-Mix Concrete Ltd.

Eastwood and Kimberlev Advertiser

The Countess of —— who was with a merry party wore nothing to indicate that she was a holder of four Scottish titles.

Scottish paper

COW SAVES A LIFE

Hauls farmer by tail
from blazing building

Sussex paper

'We saw 26 deer come down to feed,' sighed Helen Bowman, and added that they were wearing warm sweaters at the time.

Miami Herald

To taking up floor to find rat and replacing same ... 10s 6d.

Builder's invoice

The Duchess still looks quite a girl, and so does the Duke, particularly now that he has shaved off his tiny moustache.

Weekly paper

Woofy, the rough-haired terrier belonging to Mrs Perkins of Boundary Road, wags his tail at the shop doorway until Mr Bert Williams, who keeps the shop for his father, picks up the meat in his mouth and takes it home.

Norfolk paper

For his comfort the roadman has a brassière which is very nice on a cold day.

Schoolgirl's essay

Alderman Smithson said that the Council ought to be given the whole truth that there was sufficient coal in the city to last five weeks if nobody used it.

Yorkshire paper

Our 6s. Tea makes Plain Bread and Butter seem delicious

Notice in Manchester shop window

Repairs to the Town Clerk are completed and the Borough Surveyor reported that the fitters would be assembling the parts this week.

Cambrian News

Graham Stilwell, one of this year's Wimbledon heroes, was involved in another match on Saturday – his wedding. Graham, with his partner, Whipps Cross Hospital, met his lovely bride while on tour in North America three years ago.

Stratford Express

Completing an impressive ceremony, the Admiral's lovely daughter smashed a bottle of champagne over her stern as she slid gracefully down the slipways.

Provincial magazine

All this is being investigated today by the Scottish Society for the Prevention of Cruelty to Animals and Glasgow police.

Glasgow Evening Times

In an Everton attack, Royle was injured and lay writing in the centre of the field.

Middlesex paper

If you asked six friends to name the commonest bird in Britain, the odds are that nine out of ten would say the sparrow.

Weekend

Found, one set false teeth to fit black cat.

Bristol Evening Post

ACROSS a broad stubborn nose he carried a pair of gold-rimmed spectacles, a neat grey lounge suit, and a blue shirt with collar to match.

from a novel

FOR SALE – Cottage piano made in Berlin, owner getting grand.

Advert in *The Pioneer*

During the past few days three bicycles have been stolen from Exeter streets. The police consider that a bicycle thief is at work.

Western Morning News

To keep flies from marking electric light globes, smear them with camphorated oil.

Weekly paper

After Governor Baldridge watched the lion perform, he was taken to Main Street and fed twenty-five pounds of raw meat in front of the Fox Theatre.

Idaho Statesman

LOST. Evening frock and under-garments with Gladys H—— inside. Finder rewarded.

Kentucky paper

There was little Ernest Hunter, whose indescribable hat covered a head that must have knocked around the world considerably before he found it.

The Clarion

Woman wants cleaning three days a week.

Advert in *The Guardian*

Dig the ground over thoroughly and then pant.

Gardening article

The first few days the chicks were fed inside the brooder house on pieces of asbestos concrete sheets, 3 ft long by 2 ft wide.

Poultry article

The motorist stuck miles from anywhere has only himself to blame if he has not brought an up-to-date road mop.

A weekly pictorial

Most of the owner-drivers I know make a practice of washing their ears at least once a week.

Motoring paper

The skipper spat disconsolately down the engine-room ventilator and stopped the engines.

Sea story

Q. How may slightly soiled playing cards be cleaned?
A. They are made by stringing pieces of meat, quarters of onions, and two-inch pieces of bacon on sticks and broiling them over coals.

American magazine

The age limit for Girl Guides was formerly 18 years, but by general request it has now been raised to 81 years.

Local paper

THE faces of the two men were livid with rage as she quietly crumpled them up and threw them on the fire.

Short story

Colonel Marsden says that the fire was a terrible blow to him for he had spent a large sum of money on it and had extensions and improvements in view.

Yorks paper

Mr George Dobbs, of Chertsey, is very proud of the fact that he walked 50 miles on a sausage sandwich at the weekend.

Staines and Egham News

All the goods saved from the ruins was a bushel of potatoes. They escaped only in their night clothing.

Pennsylvania paper

The Chairman said the Council had never paid one penny for the oiling and washing of the Fire Brigade.

Local paper

BRITISH FLY TO DISCUSS PROBLEM PIPELINE

Headline in *The Sun*

```
   Sir, The first time I heard the cuckoo
was on April 12th.  Flying overhead from
the garden, my husband heard it before
that date.
```

Letter to *Western Gazette*

Wanted:

EDIBLE OIL TECHNOLOGIST

Advert in *The Observer*

The skirts to be worn by day are short. Some are kilted broadly and stitched to the knees.

Norfolk paper

WANTED – man to take care
of cow that does not smoke or
drink.

Advert in South Carolina paper

Five rmd house to let, two recep rooms, three bedrms, excellent kitchen, separate baths and lavs (three miles out), 15 minute bus service.

Advert in Northern paper

Before wearing black woollen stockings stand for 10 minutes in boiling water coloured with washing blue.

Laundry hint in cookery book

You really do no good by constantly scalding a child.

Women's paper

The member admitted that he was wrong in calling the man the biggest scoundrel in the village. He had forgotten himself for a moment.

Surrey paper

● Rose-trees should be carefully sprayed each morning with insecticide.　Remove all dead roots from last winter's cabbages and renew subsoil. Put into small glass jars and spread lightly on bread-and-butter.

South Indian paper

A villager will always tell the difference between a good coin and a bad one, but he cannot tell the difference between a bad coin and a good one.

Pioneer

All through the French Revolution the women ot France knitted and they dropped a stitch every time a head fell into the gelatine.

American schoolboy's essay

> SIR, Allow me to thank those electors who have promised me their kind support. I shall be unable to call upon them all and this no doubt will be appreciated by them.

Bucks paper

Can you advise me what to do with my face? I've had it for several years and it seems to get no better.

Women's weekly

L.G.S. For the delicate lingerie blouse you describe we think that you will find the water in which a quantity of unsalted rice has been boiled quite sufficient stiffening. Wait until the mixture is cold before adding the flavouring.

The Guardian

The native inhabitants produce all manner of curios, the great majority of which appear to command a ready sale among the visitors, crude and commonplace as these frequently are.

Bulawayo Chronicle

The leather bag in which he made daily trips to New York with money and papers was fastened to his shoulders like a knapsack.

New York Herald Tribune

We come now to the vexed question of dying, which is one that every woman has to consider if she lives long enough.

The Sunday Times

At Morfa Colliery, the scene of a terrible disaster years ago, props and débris fell in the workings, and then ran helter-skelter to the shaft and were drawn up pale and trembling.

The Standard

Roads constructed of this material are not subject to the dust nuisance caused to pedestrians over which motor-cars run.

Barbados Advocate

Try our patent mosquito destroyer coil, 1*s* 6*d*. It is perfectly safe for mosquitoes.

Advert in Burmese paper

 HYMN No 336
   (Congregation standing)
SERMON, 'What are you stand-
   ing for?' – Dr Fosdick.

New York church bulletin

The new automatic couplings fitted to the organ will enable Mr R—— to change his combinations without moving his feet.

Parish magazine

Bob guided her to the spinet. He took his spectacles off his beaky nose and invited Mrs Ransome to admire it. 'It's much smaller than Aunt Bertha's,' she said.

Modern Woman

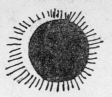

At about one o'clock when the eclipse was on the sun, I saw a most beautiful star shining very bright, and I pointed this out to three ladies who were watching the eclipse in a bath of water. Is this an unusual occurrence?

Letter in West London paper

'Mr Perkins might be able to help you,' she said, as she took down a dusty lodger from the shelf.

Weekly magazine serial

In addition to the fine work done by the Irish regiments he assured them that many a warm Irish heart beat under a Scottish kilt.

Daily paper

WANTED – A domesticated lady to live with an elderly lady to hell with the cooking and housework.

Notice in agency window

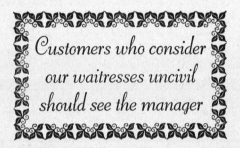

Customers who consider our waitresses uncivil should see the manager

Notice in café

The bride wore a gown of white satin featuring scooped neckline, elbow-length sleeves, and bell-shaped skirt, with a square train a few loose slates, and the ridge tiles silk veil fell from a satin head-band.

Southport Visitor

GARDENS DUG, widows washed, and chimneys swept in Tallaght area.

Advert in *Dublin Evening Herald*

At Woodford people were pouring out of buses into Epping Forest looking green and lovely.

Evening Standard

A resolution was passed which instructed Secretary Rigg to write to the department of militia asking for (*a*) the names of the shoe-makers who were catering for the feeding of the troops, (*b*) the names of the cooks and caterers supplying the boots and shoes.

Winnipeg Free Press

STEAMER COLLIDES IN FOG

The Norwegian steamer *Gaea* put into dock at Dover today with her bows damaged as the result of a collision with an unknown Football at Woolwich and Fulham.

Pall Mall Gazette

Our photograph shows a typical Poole street scene, though actually it was taken in Lymington last summer.

West Country paper

Again for an instant she raised those wonderful eyes to his. He studied the thickness of the lashes as they fell once more to her lap.

Truth

FOR SALE – Baker's business, good trade, large oven, present owner been in it seventeen years.

Kent paper

Then they waved to their friends with one hand and chewed sandwiches with the other.

Norfolk paper

She sat huddled in a chair, covering her ears with crossed legs.

Short story

Then it spread to Liz, who clapped a hand over her mouth above blue eyes that watered with silent laughter.

from *Nothing* by Henry Green

POLICE MISTAKE AT WALSALL

Innocent man released

Birmingham Daily Mail

Keeping all food under cover is the first step towards ridding the house of aunts.

Albany Journal

The raiders took about £600 in cash. 'They left nothing untouched, the whole place was a shabgm', selM'bolaletaoin in a shambles,' Mr Higgins said.

North Berks Herald

Porter rubbed his nose, wondering what it would sound like, and if it would appear as it had twenty years before when he'd taken part in it all.

from *Light Cavalry Action* by John Harris

The spare key to the First Aid Room is available in the First Aid Room.

Notice in government department

The plumbers have finished their part of the contract at the new township, and there now remains only the plumbing to be done.

Australian paper

Mr and Mrs Wally Burman of Sioux Falls have just arrived at the Lindau home where they will be housepests for several days.

Minnesota paper

TURKEY CARPET for sale good condition the property of a lady too large for her rooms.

Advert in Scottish paper

My wife took an instant dislike to my guests and went out of her way to make painful scones.

Evening paper

The service ended with the singing of the good old hymn: 'All police that on the earth do dwell.'

Canadian paper

Discovered at 5.06 AM the flames starting on the third floor of the Midwest Salvage Co, spread so rapidly that the first firemen on the scene were driven back to safety and leaped across three streets to ignite other buildings.

Cincinnati Times Star

Fire of unknown origin completely destroyed the home and contents of Mr and Mrs Salford.

Corona (California) paper

Princess B— wore a white and gold lace gown which she'd saved for the occasion. To give you an idea how elaborate it was, the centre-piece was a mirror $13\frac{1}{2}$ feet long with elaborate matching candelabra of fruit-baskets.

Los Angeles Mirror

Mr Sagara noticed a little cubicle that was vacant. He sat at the table and studied the menu through spectacles and clenched teeth.

Evening paper story

WAITRESSES for breakfast: 7 AM to 11 AM. St James' Court Hotel, Buckingham Gate, SW1. Apply Head Waiter.

Advert in South London Press

Ears Pierced Whilst You Wait

Notice in Somerset jeweller's shop

... and a few moments after the Countess had broken the traditional bottle of champagne on the bows of the noble ship, she slid slowly and gracefully down the slipway, entering the water with scarcely a splash.

Essex paper

BABY SHOW – Best Baby under Six Months; Best Baby under Twelve Months; Best Baby under Two Years; Best Baby under Three Years. Rules for Exhibitors: All Exhibits become the property of the Committee as soon as staged, and will be sold for the benefit of the Hospital at the termination of the exhibition.

Exhibition programme

TREATED LIKE DOG BY WIFE HUSBAND COOKED FOR 30 YEARS

The Daily Telegraph

An exciting fire broke out yesterday on the premises of the Society for Promoting Christian Knowledge in Northumberland Avenue.

Daily Mirror

Don't Kill Your Wife with Work

Let Electricity Do It

Poster in Willesden

Farmer S—— wishes to thank sincerely all those who assisted in the burning of his barn.

Suhler Intelligenz-Blatt

For nearly three-quarters of an hour the fire blazed without any real abatement, and it was only when it had burned itself out that there was any real diminution in the intensity of the flames.

Dundee Advertiser

Q. What is the best method of cooking eggs to preserve the most vitamins?

A. Experiments have led to the conclusion that the best method of cooking eggs for vitamin retention is scrambling followed by boiling and frying.

Boston Traveller

They were all delighted to have Miss Benson back amongst them. Their best wishes would go with her next week when she set out for her holiday, and they all hoped she would return with

MEASLES AND WHOOPING-COUGH

Scottish paper

Yesterday in this column the wording appeared: 'fellows in the back row, among whom I was with'. That was a typographical error. It was originally written: 'fellows in the back row, among whom I was which'.

We trust that makes everything clear.

San Francisco Chronicle

MATRESSES REMADE
PILLOWS CLEANED
New ticks supplied at reasonable prices.

Advert in *Yorkshire Post*

Voluntary workers
put in Church heating plant

The Barnet Press

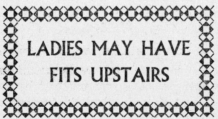

Shanghai tailor's sign

Granting a decree to a wife at Swansea Assizes, Mr Commissioner O. Temple-Morris said her husband wrote her a letter which should not have been sent to a dog.

News of the World

Said a Farnborough shopkeeper, 'The Council is pulling the bread and butter out from under our feet'.

Hants paper

The bus came to rest with its front two feet in the air.

Sheffield Star

HALL with kitchen and toilet (can seat 100 persons), or could be converted for dwelling house.

Edinburgh Evening News and Dispatch

Whichever method is used for cleaning the dog's paws, make sure that the paw is thoroughly washed with luke-warm water and is thoroughly dried. Spread with cream cheese. Place 2 or 3 asparagus tips on each and sprinkle on a little cayenne papper.

South Wales Gazette and Newport News

We would draw your attention to our excellent delivery service, which covers most of the town with fish three times a day.

Tradesman's circular

Humidity is perhaps the distinctively Christian virtue.

Indian paper

On Saturday night at 8 PM the annual potato-pie supper will be held. The subject of the sermon on Sunday morning will be 'A night of horror'.

Church paper

Evening subject: 'What is hell like?'
Come and hear our new organ

Cumberland church notice-board

Our picture shows the Archbishop of York tapping the foundation stone with the Bishop of Barking.

Caption in daily paper

So they set off. The Chief Constable with his brown cane tucked under his right arm. Chief Superintendent C.F. Broughton next – carrying nothing. Detective-Inspector E.G. Westmile wore just a gasmask.

North London paper

The three occupants of the vehicle were killed, the first two outright, and the third on arrival at hospital.

Translation from *Depêche du Midi*

A fixture that has brought nothing but defeat since 1949 was won at last by the shooting of two Football League forwards.

Daily Mail

The bride made her own wedding gown – a classic style in white brocade. Her train was the 6.15 PM from Redhill.

Surrey Mirror and County Post

The manufacturers of this sock MUST be washed in LUKEWARM water, NOT HOT, and well rinsed to remove soap.

Instructions with Pearlustra socks

The competitors were in no way upset by the cold north-east wind blowing on the diving-board from the four corners of the earth.

Daily Mail

Ickes declared: 'It should be thoroughly understood that the Solid Fuels Administration is not trying to convert anthracite consumers to the use of bituminous coal. We are trying to convert anthracite consumers to the use of bituminous coal.'

Springfield (Mass.) *Evening Union*

At Caxton Hall the conference was resumed of Municipal authorities interested in the conversation of old fruit, sardine, and salmon tins.

Birmingham Daily Mail

The famous composer, Karl Maria von Weber, was born in Eutin, Oldenburg, in 1786, a few weeks after the production in Germany, at Covent Garden, of his opera *Oberon*.

Indiana paper

Zanuck, in his speech, showed great humility and told briefly of his beginning here in our midst. But he didn't reflect his early struggles; how, when he wrote and wrote and got one rejection after the other and could not even get into a studio, he had to take a job down at Wilmington catching hot rivets in the shipbuilding plant to eat.

Hollywood Reporter

SERVICE HAND. Mon–Fri. 10.30–
3.30. £7 to serve waitresses from
the hot plate. Tel: MIN 9999.

Evening Standard

'Alan broke his leg in two places a month ago at
nursery school – we don't know how,' his father laughed.

Slough Observer

Usually the annual effort is a sale of work and a concert, but this year so as not to put too great a strain on
supporters, a concert and a sale of work have been ar-
ranged.

Exeter Express and Echo

He stopped and re-lit his cigarette with a great light
in his eyes.

Scottish paper

Palace's defence was suspect during quick breakaways
and a poor back pass from Blyth brought Jackson out
of his area to kick off Treacy's toes.

The Evening News

IT'S THEIR SHOW – Mr and Mrs Alvan W. Sulloway, of Concord, NH, librettist and composer of *Winner Take All*. She writes music with her three little boys on her hands.

Boston Globe

It is upsetting somewhat the plans of the high German officers who are arranging things from afar through telescopes down which they shout their orders.

Liverpool Daily Post

The officer in command kept his head and cleverly ordered his men to keep behind it as it moved forward.

Daily paper

Tomorrow week the Canadian regimental doctors will be deposited for safe keeping in Bristol Cathedral.

Bristol paper

LOST – vicinity Milton–Cameron roads, brownish black cat; light inside tail tip.

Advert in local paper

A great amount of useful information was given by the demonstrator. The height of her talk was how to bottle fruit without fruit, which needless to say attracted much attention.

Parish magazine

To make a piece of boiled bacon really delicious, add to the water a teaspoonful of vinegar, a small bit of nutmeg, and a couple of gloves.

Women's magazine

As I strolled through the car park I was depressed by the condition of some of the vehicles. Some of the owners did not appear to have washed their ears for weeks.

South African paper

B—— School. Wanted in January – Experienced man to take almost entire responsibility for the lowest form of boys.

Manchester paper

WANTED IMMEDIATELY

a woman for boiling down

Apply Blake Potted Meat Company

Advert in New Zealand paper

LOST. Friday night between Market Square and Dimsdale Avenue, Black and White Terrier. Name and address on collar of owner.

Advert in local paper

He looked at her with infinite tenderness. 'I know all about it,' he said.

She covered her face with her hands and cried brokenly. But, coming closer, he put both hands on her shoulders, and lifted her tea-stained face to his.

Tasmanian Courier Annual

The bride, who was given away by her father, wore a dress of pale bridegroom. She was attended by the hat, and carried a bouquet, the gift of the pink taffeta silk and a large dark blue bridegroom's two little nieces.

Kentish paper

Here the couple stood, facing the floral setting and exchanged cows.

California paper

Until further notice, no steam-roller, steam-wagon, heavy lorry, or charabanc, will be allowed to run over the bride.

Bedford paper

IF IT'S SWEETS TRY US
The best is none too good.

Confectioner's advert

Sir, In reply to Mr Yarham's letter in Saturday's *Eastern Daily Press*, I would like to point out that the cuckoo heard by my niece on Saturday week and the one I heard and saw on Monday was not riding a cycle when I saw it fly out of a tree.

Eastern Daily Press

WHY BREAK YOUR CHINA WASHING UP?

Do it automatically in a dishwasher!
From John R. Fordham, Epping.
Phone 33   Established 1923

Advert in *Surrey Mirror*

A two-year-old Sheffield boy, hospital today after swallowing Graham Cotton was taken to aspirin tablets at his home.

Sheffield paper

Boys' stretchable T-shirts are Fashion's new snap-on clips that transform your daytime glasses into evening gaiety.

Advert in *San Diego Tribune*

James Ward, RA, gained the prize, but being too large to hang his painting was rolled up and placed in Chelsea Hospital.

Trade publication

The easiest way to clean a cereal cooker is to turn it upside down in a pan of white flannel laid with the soft side on the inside and quilted on the machine.

Oxford Times

To emphasize the shape of the eyes, pencil in a fine brown line actually following the growth of the lashes. Mascara must be made into a nice creamy consistency and lower lashes made up as well with lemon curd and ice the top with lemon water icing, or sprinkle icing sugar on top.

Greenock Telegraph

Sir,
It gives me great pleasure to be able to tender you my good wishes for the future progress of your most popular morning paper, *The Yorkshire Observer*, without which I should not be satisfied, for it is half my breakfast.

Letter in *The Yorkshire Observer*

Mrs Thomas Jennings' classes for children of pre-kindergarten age will be resumed on Mondays, Wednesdays and Fridays, from 9 to 12 o'clock. A slight smack will be served about 10.30.

Connecticut paper

An assistant master of the Bromley Road Schools submitted an application for leave of absence in order to attend a special vaccination course in geography.

Beckenham Journal

Word was received last week that Mrs Gertrude Higgins, teacher of the 36th Street School, was severely bitten by a dog on the school grounds. Principal Gail Mahoney observed that it could just as easily have been a child.

Los Angeles South-West News-Press

BLOODHOUND IN CHILD HUNT FOUND, PICKING BLACKBERRIES

Daily Express

Mr and Mrs Remington Taylor, of Verona, formerly of Ithaca, were weakened guests of Mrs J. H. Barron, of 145 Cascadilla Park.

Ithaca Journal

Road conditions in the New Forest were the worst known for years. In several places the roads were lined with cats unable to climb the snow-covered hills.

Sussex paper

If you are having dancing and don't want your carpet ruined, to save taking it up, turn it upside down.

Caterham Times

One day at lunch we saw a cat with something in its mouth climb one wall. The cat was carrying a kitchen.

Essex paper

THE
GREYHOUND INN

*An old coaching inn dating
from the fifteenth century*

NO COACHES

Inn sign

He heard the stable clock strike the hour, and a few moments later Monica in the doorway.

Woman

He is now being kept alive by an artificial respirator and massive doses of rugs.

Nelson Evening Mail

At a meeting held in the institute last Wednesday, Mrs Davis was won by Mrs J. Hawker.

Darlington and Stockton Times

THIS ROAD IS CLOSED TO
ALL VEHICULAR TRAFFIC EXCEPT
GOVERNMENT VEHICLES AND
THOSE BELONGING TO PERSONS
HAVING BUSINESS AT PIRBRIGHT
AND NOT EXCEEDING 126in. IN
HEIGHT WHO MAY USE IT AT
THEIR OWN RISK

Sign at entrance to
Pirbright Camp

K——'s Bridal Hire. Brides from £5, with all accessories. Also bridesmaids any style made to measure.

Leyton and Leytonstone Guardian

To move the cabin, push button of wishing floor. If the cabin should enter more persons, each one should press number of wishing floor. Driving is then going alphabetically by natural order. Button retaining pressed position shows received command for visiting station.

Notice in Belgrade hotel lift

On the evening of May 13th, at about 7 o'clock, travelling north and giving off a roaring sound, my husband and I both saw clearly some silver coloured objects in the sky.

Letter in *Milwaukee Journal*

A tight hat can be stretched. First damp the head with steam from a boiling kettle . . .

Scots paper

CHILD GETS MORE MILK
WHEN COOKED IN THE PORRIDGE

Canadian paper

Don't risk infecting the baby with a dirty feeding bottle teat. When the baby has finished its bottle drop it in a saucepan of water and boil it.

Women's magazine

WANTED, maid for mousework, four in family.

> Advert in Toronto paper

Seats – see under Members.

> Index to House of Commons
> official report (*Hansard*)

WANTED – Sports leather coat for lady in perfect condition.

> *Nippon Times*

To close these special envelopes, first wet the gum, then insert the tongue into lock and draw until you hear it snap.

> Lloyds Bank instructions

Owing to a plague of wasps in the Sheffield district, farmers have had to stop harvest operations to take wasps wasp nests before they could gather in their wasps.

> *Edinburgh Evening Dispatch*

About a month ago a long red radish reached us from a reader the normal size of a carrot.

> *Amateur Gardening*

Horse and rider came with great force to the ground. Mr Climping escaped with a broken neck, which he had given £25 for a short time previously.

Lawloit Times

The tiger came towards me bellowing and grunting, and when he got opposite the screen he gave one of those fearful coughs which only the man who has been close to such a beast can appreciate. It was eleven feet long.

Evening Standard

Once this work is completed, the stained windows will be put back into their frames and the pews will be replaced. Good progress is being made by the workmen of Messrs Jackson, Builders, McGregor, Marshall, Brown, Murray (Captain), and Thompson. Reserves: Green and Morrison. Kick-off 2.15.

Northumberland paper

Photographs of the Church and the Vicar (interior and exterior) may be had of the Verger.

Notice in Berkshire church

Marinade the steak in the sauce for at least two hours, then cook a hot grill, basting with the sauce at frequent intervals. Alternatively, pour off sauce after marinading, heat separately, and let your guests pour it over themselves.

Recipe in Ohio newspaper

A thief went to work in the changing room at Burton-wood Rugby Club. Honey was taken from the pockets of five players.

Ashton and Haydock Reporter

BANANAS IN SYRUP

Heat in an enamel-lined saucepan some red-currant jelly and raspberry jam dissolved in water, making a pint in all. When it boils, drop into it a dozen peeled tomatoes.

Weekly paper

 **Order Now Your Summers Suit because is big rush we will execute all customers in strict rotation**

Sign in Jordan tailor's shop

Her eyes lit up, fluttered, met his, dropped to the floor, went back to the jewels. He picked them up, held them for a moment, then handed them back to her with a tender smile.

from a short story

£1 REWARD. Lost, an Octagonal Lady's Gold Wristlet Watch.

Advert in Wigan paper

The public house is a one-storey building and the occupants were sleeping upstairs.

The Evening News

The principal thing to remember when preparing a fork supper is to select only food which can be eaten comfortably on a plate with a fork. In the winter, hot bouillon or clear soup is always popular and can well be included.

Sunday paper

My daughter-in-law has the same name as that of law insists that she was taught by it belongs to this era even if it was his father, Madam. I hardly think her another to tell a widow, whose proper. Will you explain?

Letter in Manchester paper

At the astonishment by missing a putt of not short fourth caused a gasp of quite eighteen inches.

Sporting paper

The last wicket fell just before lunchtime. After the interval a very pleasing improvement in the dimensions of the spectators was to be seen.

East Anglian Daily Times

What is more beautiful for a blonde to wear for formal dances than white tulle? My answer – and I'm sure you will agree with me – is 'Nothing'.

Worcester (Mass.) *Evening Gazette*

Deryk stood watching her, his hands in his pockets, a splendid specimen of English manhood in his white flannels, his tennis racket in his strong brown hands.

Story in church paper

Cambridge University has decided to confer honorary degrees on all except students seeking first-class horrors, for whom the examinations will be held as usual.

Bucks paper

Much has been written on the subject of rose cultivation. Let us take soil preparation first. You will want a loam containing plenty of humans and good drainage.

San Francisco Examiner

At a recent fire in the south of Scotland, twenty-four hens, a ton of coals, and a quantity of potatoes were burned alive.

Scottish paper

LOST, Tabby cat, male, answers to John. Reward (one black eye).

Advert in Devonshire paper

The girls of St Monica's school have assisted in the preparation of three hampers for needy pensioners, making the cakes, curd, mincemeat, sweets, etc, themselves. Six recipients died during the year.

Charity report

If You Don't Say
MRS GLOBUS CHOCOLATE PUDDING
Is the Finest You Ever Tasted
TEAR UP THE CASHIER AND WALK OUT

Menu of a Baltimore restaurant

Confirming my call on the 2nd instant, I
do assure you that the spots on the enamel
of your cooker will not deteriorate. If
they do during the next three years the
Board would exchange them without charge.

Letter from Gas Board

Ten sampans were entered, the boats being gaily
decorated with flags. The result was a very amusing race
in which the winner passed the post only a length behind
the second.

Hongkong Overseas Mail

I was terrified ... There was the tiger crouching, ready
to bounce.

Short story

The forwards shot hard and often but never straight
till at last Hill decided to try his head. It came off first time.

Kent paper

THIS WILL BE A SHOW WHICH YOU MUST NOT FAIL TO MISS

Advert in Rangoon paper

The Concert held in the Good Templars' Hall was a great success ... Special thanks are due to the Vicar's daughter, who laboured the whole evening at the piano, which as usual fell upon her.

South African paper

The great white elephant which is slowly emerging from the chrysalis at the end of Sepoy Lines has yet to be opened.

Malayan paper

TODAY'S GOLF HINT. If your driving is not so good as usual try to get the left hip and clubhead to strike the ball at the same instant.

Provincial paper

Under the baton of Mr S. Rutherford the Cosmopolitan Club Orchestra provided musical numbers. Miss Ivy Parker's outstanding features convulsed the audience.

Gisborne Herald

Fugue in E Flat . . . . . Major Bach

Concert programme

BLOTTING PAPER WILL NOT BE PROVIDED UNTIL THE PUBLIC STOPS TAKING IT AWAY

Notice in a village post office

Thank God we have a Prime Minister who does not always wait to cross a bridge until he comes to it.

Letter in *The Times*

Mr John McFadden was re-appointed to wind, oil, and keep the Town Clerk in order.

Irish paper

FOR SALE. Wicked Bath Chair, and good mahogany Bed Table.

Kentish paper

PLEASE NOTE. YOU can order our rings by post.
☆   State size or enclose string tied
               round finger.

Advert in Yorks paper

Why is it that tenants of Council property are treated
like so many prawns on a chess board?

Louth Standard

He broke into the building with an older boy, and they then splattered the walls with floor, ransacked teachers' desks, and one beheaded the school paste, tipped treacle on the goldfish with a paper guillotine.

Slough Observer

The title of the film 'PLINK PLONK PLINK' (F 52377), registered on June 7th, 1967, has been corrected to read 'PLINK PLUNK PLINK'.

Board of Trade Journal

Fourteen-year-old Victor Harris has passed with credit two of the recent Royal Academy of Music piano examinations.

For failing to stop he was fined £5.

Darlington and Stockton Times

Railway tickets of the Sunday Route March will be issued at drill hall on Wednesday; members who cannot attend please apply to Cdr-Sgt, stating which line they will travel by.

Rifle Brigade Battalion Orders

The sense of duty on the part of the sailor at the lookout was the most sublime I have ever known. He stood at his post without a thought of deserting it, though buried by tons of ice.

The Standard

One of the handiest men around the huge bombers at Hill Air Force base is 80-pound Shorty Osborne. Only 5 inches tall, Stanley Osborne can crawl into tight places in bomber wings and tails to make repairs.

Indiana paper

If my mother were alive today to see shops opened and mixed bathing on the Sabbath, she would turn in her grave.

Letter in Irish paper

WRECKER SERVICE – Member's car will be pulled out of ditch, or stuck in mud, or involved in accident free of charge, within radius of 10 miles.

Dallas Automobile Club notice

Comfortable home offered to two gentlemen, or otherwise.

Advert in Surrey paper

Quiet, clean gentleman seeks comfortable room where he can cook himself on a spirit stove.

Münchner Neueste Nachrichten

Bedsitting room to let for gent; terms 85/– meekly.

Advert in local paper

THIS place is the preferred resort for those wanting solitude. People searching for such solitude are in fact flocking here from all corners of the globe.

Swiss resort prospectus

Club members are requested not to drive their cars into the club garage when it is full.

Notice at Irish golf course

The Christening ceremony was performed by Lady Maclay, wife of the Shipping Controller. Thousands of people saw her go down the ways, and cheers were raised as she took the water without the slightest hitch.

Daily News

After all, we are largely as nature made us, and Governor Smith's smile was born with him, just as were his liking for children and his derby hat.

Omaha Evening World-Herald

Mayor Bonner reported $3,456.00 collected as fines and costs in his Court during the month of May.

Building Commissioner Smith reported $82.50 collected by him for permits from April 16th to May 21st.

Both the Mayor and the Commissioner have left for Canada for a short vacation.

Bogota (Texas) *News*

If you were writing a letter to a member of the Cabinet of the United States, how would you address him?

'My dead Mr Secretary,' is the most acceptable form of address.

Cleveland Press

In 'The Night is Departing' chorus, a base lead was missed, partly because one of the singers was, I noticed, so deaf that he could not see the conductor.

Berkshire paper

If the patient faints when standing up he collapses on to the ground.

First-aid manual

The engagement is announced between John Christian, eldest son of Mr and Mrs Andreas, and Violent Jean, elder daughter of Mr and Mrs Benson, Kinrosshire.

Ramsey Courier

'I got something off my chest today that's been hanging over my head for some time. That's behind me now, thank goodness.'

Film star on BBC interview

Miss Hazel Foster's gladioli garden has been attracting considerable attention of late. She spends many hours among her large collection of pants.

Pennsylvania paper

Sipping hot tea, as many players do, Andrews served, drove and volleyed with brilliant energy and control.

Sussex paper

In Elmfield Avenue, Teddington, last Saturday, cigarette ash falling in the cat's box caused a small fire. Little damage was done and the blaze was put out by the occupier.

Surrey Comet

WANTED in Abingdon – Between £3,350–£3,850, available for modern home with three bedrooms and garage or space for schoolmaster.

Advert in *Oxford Mail*

Mr Jones was elected and has accepted the office of People's Churchwarden. We could not get a better man!

from a parish magazine

Miss Wilkinson, in black satin, discarded a shawl at the swing doors which she had been wearing to ward off the chilliness of the early morning. She seemed bewildered.

Liverpool paper

At weekends Rosemary cycles 'usually to Portsmouth'. What does she do when she gets home? She strips and overhauls her bicycle.

Evening Standard

A quarter of an hour before the start Hancock scored an unconverted try for Bath.

Sunday paper

STATE MENTAL INSTITUTION
FOR ALL UP TO 18 IS URGED

Philadelphia Enquirer

In his annual report, Dr Porter, Medical Officer of the County of ——, deplored the fact that oatmeal porridge, a splendid article of diet, was becoming unfashionable, and is supplanted by silk stockings.

Irish paper

Fearing a fracture of the jaw, the doctor had to stitch up his left eyelid.

Translated from Ouest-France

> NOTE – Bring this card with
> you or you will not be seen.

Appointment card, Edgware General
Hospital

WOMAN FALLS THREE STOREYS AS SHE WATERS FLOWERS

Long Island Daily Star

She appears as a circus clown, juggling with three balls, a pianist, and a dancer.

Daily Express

Let there be no misunderstanding. A mating of two champion sheep-dogs is more likely to produce a super Border Collie than the mating of two champion cattle or horses.

The Scotsman

● The season for grass fires seems to have arrived, so stamp out that cigarette-end before you throw it down.

Herne Bay Press

Miss Yolande Lessard, sister of the bride, was maid of honour and wore a white nylon skirt, matching ostrich plumes in her hair and carried a royal-blue brother of the bride, and Marcel. The bridegroom was attended by his velvet muff covered with pink roses.

Portland Press Herald

Mrs Smithson - - - cheque and magnifying glass.

from a list of wedding presents

Twin baby boys, aged 12 months, arrived at Folkestone yesterday unconcerned, after a rough Channel crossing in a wooden box fitted with cushions.

Sunday paper

To prevent suffocation, babies should never be allowed to lie face down on their backs, said officials of the Canadian Mothercraft Society.

Canadian paper

Lady offers stylish well-cut apparel, reducing corset, waist 29, for Alsatian dog.

Women's paper

The flames spread over hills and valleys, destroying all vegetation, driving foxes and rabbits to leave their nesting grounds, their eggs being destroyed.

Newcastle paper

They took with them an Irish terrier dog and a brown sheep dog – both pets. Both were wearing horn-rimmed glasses.

Manchester paper

During the interval the huge park was full of the local gentry that arrived in hundreds of cars and ate excellent home-made cakes under an enormous marquise.

Manchester paper

The party went by way of Ockendon, Bulphan, and Laindon, and the sea was reached about 1 o'clock. The tide was out, a thoughtful arrangement by the secretary.

Local paper

Two women trying to cross the street near 22nd St, Bellaire, turned wrong side out and ribs were broken.

West Virginia paper

There is a sub-department of Scotland Yard which looks after Kings and visiting potentates, Cabinet Ministers, spies, anarchists, and other undesirables.

South London paper

DUCHESS TO
RACE GREYHOUNDS

Headline in Northampton paper

PC Thorley, who apprehended Jackson, said he be-
came very violent at the police station where he threw
several coppers on the table which was damaged.

Wiltshire paper

In a raid on Partington Railway Station during the weekend, thieves stole four dozen pencils and three dozen ball-point pen refills.

They told the *Guardian* that their headmaster was very pleased with their success and the honour it reflected on the school.

Sale and Stretford Guardian

We can safely say that there is no repair job necessary on a car than cannot be executed more efficiently than by us.

Advert in Rhodesian paper

The font so generously presented by Mrs Smith will be set in position at the East end of the Church. Babies may now be baptized at both ends.

Surrey paper

The death took place on Friday morning of Sodium Phenylmethylpyrazolonamidomethansulphonate.

Western Daily Press

Councillor Bertrand supported the street lamp at the corner of Truro Lane.

Lake's Falmouth Packet

The uncertain character of the weather makes it highly undesirable that the Prime Minister should venture out before his convalescence is practically complete. Many callers continue to make inquiries at 10 Downing Street. Yesterday Lord L—— was among the number, pressing his throat, throwing him to the ground.

Aberdeen Free Press

This butter, manufactured from the best cream, will stand any high temperature if kept in a cool place.

Bombay catalogue

HEALTH BISCUITS
Nice and tasty
Handled by our 55 salesmen daily

Advert in *Montreal Star*

BLANK'S NERVE TONIC
drives away nervy symptoms, gives power of brain and body.
LEAVES BEHIND irritability, indigestion, rheumatism, neuralgia, hysteria, etc.

Advert in a timetable

Presiding Superior Judge Ruston Garton will be the speaker, and he will tell some humorous anecdotes while doing some underwater spear-fishing.

Santa Ana (California) *Register*

After using your ointment my face started to clear up at once, and after using two jars it was gone altogether.

Advert in Bristol paper

A familiar question was re-opened – how Sunday School children are to be attached to the Church, and once more the use of adhesive stamps was recommended.

New Zealand Church News

GREAT SERVICE TO EDUCATION
Mr Eric Jones resigns
from County Committee

Salisbury Journal

Every Friday, some weeks to come, the railways will run cheap excursions to Scotland and several other towns in the North of England.

Cambridge Chronicle

Please excuse John from
school today as father's
ill and the pig
has to be fed

Letter to schoolmaster

The explosion occurred in the chemical laboratory late on Thursday afternoon. One or two boys are suffering slightly from buns.

Local paper

The Cuckoo is a bird that lays other birds' eggs in its own nest and *viva voce*.

Schoolgirl's essay

LOOE WATER SPORTS ASSOCIATION

MONTHLY REGATTA

6.0 PM. Water Polo. Friendly match (if possible).

Notice in Looe

Concrete Block Machines – Really you would like our newest machine. It produces slabs and hollow blocks of every thickness. Made entirely out of our own heads.

Smallholder

LOOK AT OUR BARGAINS

and save your money

Notice in London shop

He has a curious action, for he appears to get a little mixed up with his feet as he reaches the crease, and finally delivers the ball with the wrong one.

Essex paper

The letter pointed out that whereas there were definite allocations of oranges from time to time, the supply of demons was very short.

Northants paper

In the next compartment was the wife of a prominent politician, off to the Riviera. Her husband, seeing her off, looked wistfully after the train as it pulled out of the station with its heavy load.

Daily Mail

Alderman Johnston moved that pending the passing of the street by-law, that all vehicles on Columbia Street be required to keep to the left going up and to the right going down.

The British Columbian

From first to last the grip that he maintained over his large audience was shown by the keen attention with which they hung upon his words and the deep silence with which their bursts of silence alternated.

Westminster Gazette

Margaret Lockwood. Her chin is absolutely right. It forms a gentle graceful point, balanced between wide eyes.

Weekly News, Birmingham

Mrs Grace Wright is being wired for electricity, which will be a great improvement and add considerably to her value to the community.

Medina Sentinel

When a sheep is seriously cut or otherwise injured, the sheep shall immediately report the fact to the person in charge of the shed.

Otago Daily Times

Household hint: Ink can more easily be removed from a white tablecloth before it is spilled than after.

Provincial paper

Another fur hint: if you want a fur to wear well, select one that will stand hard wear.

Fashion note

Alice paused, and, to hide her confusion, busied herself adjusting ornaments on the mantelpiece which need no adjusting. Then she turned her sweet flour-like face towards him.

Short story

A dog, alleged to be ferocious, which bit a woman in Alderney recently, was given another chance by the Court last Friday.

Guernsey Evening Press

An address was delivered by the Rev R. K. Williamson, whilst a solo was sung by Master Sandy Duff.

Scottish paper

Mrs Clyde Thomas of Pemberton fell downstairs at her home this morning breaking her myhodududududududuosy and suffered painful injuries.

Ohio paper

Customers should note that complaints of incivility on the part of any member of our staff will be severely dealt with

Notice in shop

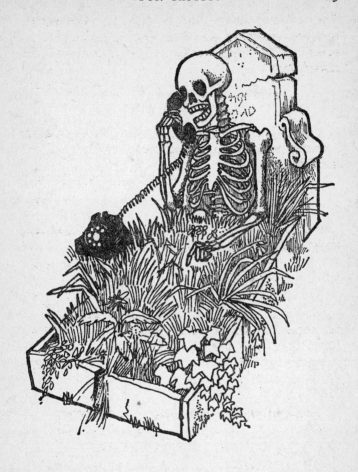

Will anyone who would like their graves attended to in the cemetery get into touch with the Secretary, Rev F. W. Thomas.

Cambridge paper

Like all papers written by people following an infinite end, the welter of have and have not, with regard to what may, if by any chance it ever, though it should, of course, is a little confusing.

Stockport Advertiser

Slough Borough babies have their big chance at the baby show. Entries can be made on the ground and during the evening the last eight will contest the Berks and Bucks darts championship.

Windsor, Slough & Eton Express

I oiled up the cylinders well and also checked over the ignition system, including a spirited performance of 'We came from the mountains' by Bach, and the sparking plugs. What do you think causes the engine to run unevenly?

Query in a motoring journal

All the bridesmaids wore red noses.

Birmingham paper

The hymns 'Love Divine' and 'O Perfect Love' were sung whilst the organist played a Wedding March.

Surrey paper

SCHOOLMASTER'S ILLNESS. Mr Francis Jameson who has undergone an operation in a London hospital, is going on satisfactorily. The hospital escaped damage.

Leighton Buzzard Observer

It is generally agreed that human beings acquire sleeping sickness from biting flies.

The Pioneer

BEWARE!
TO TOUCH THESE WIRES IS INSTANT DEATH

*Anyone found doing so
will be prosecuted*

Signboard

Mr Johnson was pinned to the ground receiving injuries to his right leg, body and shoulder. What was most trying of all, his lighted cigarette rested on the side of his cheek, near his eye, and he could not move it.

Look out for the repeat performance.

Yorkshire paper

PEDIGREE Alsatian Pup Pies, price 10 guineas each.

Advert in weekly paper

COME IN YOUR THOUSANDS

The hall holds five hundred

Concert bill

The doctor looked closely at the woman's face. 'It's a most peculiar thing,' he murmured.

Short story

The bride looked charming. She carried a bouquet of white roses and carnations and the bridegroom.

Local paper

There have been times when I used to follow a lonely white-eye in the forest, singing lustily all the time, hopping from tree to tree, as though calling for a mate.

American Cage-bird

After the accident Mr Jones and his wife were treated for abrasions of the left hip and contusions of both arms. Mrs Platt was treated at General Hospital for a laceration of her right rear leg.

Philadelphia paper

THIS IS THE GATE OF HEAVEN ENTER YE ALL BY THIS DOOR

This door is kept locked because of the draught

Notice at Cumberland church

LEARN TO DRIVE
AS YOU WATCH TV

Headline in *The Sun*

Unfortunately the Prime Minister had left before the debate began. Otherwise he would have heard some caustic comments on his absence.

Liverpool paper

A jumble sale will be held in the Parish Room on Saturday September 27th. This is a chance to get rid of anything that is not worth keeping but is too good to throw away. Don't forget to bring your husbands.

St Ambrose (Lancs) *Parish Magazine*

Mrs Carter will not be 'at home' to her friends today. PIGS.

Argentine paper

Like Adela, he had dark brown hair, with enormous black eyebrows, a moustache, and a short beard.

from *A Marriage of Inconvenience* by Thomas Cobb

My wife is passionately fond of flowers and I always give her a punch on her birthday.

Letter in local paper

He went across to the fireplace and stood with his back to its warmth, staring into the fire with unseeing eyes.

Short story

She raised her head, startled, and stared at a young boy who was smiling at her. Spread around her was a sun-flooded valley where buttercups nodded lazily in the summer breeze and tranquil cows chewed solemnly at her elbow.

Western Family Magazine

The accuracy of the England bowling was shown by the fact that R—— was at the wicket for twenty minutes before snoring.

Evening paper

Dear Mum,

just a card to say I arrived alrite and if you don't know my address write and arsk me for it and I will send it to you.

Love, Alfie.

Letter from a cadet in camp

A carpet was stolen last night from Ryde Council building. Measuring almost 6 feet square, the thief has baffled council officers.

Australian paper

Ghana is to change over to driving on the right. The change will be made gradually.

Ghana paper

INSTRUCTIONS

Pour a teaspoonful of the shampoo into the palm of each hand . . .

Label on bottle

This summer the Graham family – father, mother and teenage daughter – will move into the bungalow which they have planned and built themselves from books borrowed from their local library.

Sunday Express

Dear Madam,

With reference to your blue raincoat, our manufacturers have given the garment in question a thorough testing, and find that it is absolutely waterproof. If you will wear it on a dry day, and then take it off and examine it you will see that our statement is correct.

Your obedient servants,
BLANK & COMPANY, Drapers

WANTED, new pair of football boots, for a good young Fox-terrier dog.

Advert in *Our Dogs*

Late that same evening after a vain search all round the village, Mary found the dog dead in the garden. She curried the body indoors.

Short story

Make certain of getting the best of everything by sending to G——.
We advise you to buy the best, for even then it is not too good.

Capetown outfitter's advert

You may imagine it is impossible to obtain a good, serviceable suit for 15 gns. Buy one from us and be convinced.

Advert in Manchester paper

Wash beets very clean, then boil. When done, swim out into a pan of cold water and slip the skins off with the fingers.

Bo

At next Wednesday's children's party it is expected that in two hours 300 children will consume 1,800 sandwiches and 900 fancy cakes, gallons of milk and tea, pounds of butter and a fishfryer, a plumber, a schoolmaster, and a railway inspector.

Yorkshire Gazette

30,000 pigeons were released filling the air with the flutter of a million wings.

Commentary in a news film

Edward Slater broke his arm last week. It was a decided success and many expressed the wish that it might be an annual affair.

American paper

As a matter of fact, Jackson calmly waited to be fetched, and I fear his suffering was not so great as people thought. He dislocated a hip hip hurrah, and was soon all right again.

Provincial paper

Cycling along a route used by Livingstone when he first saw Lake Tanganyika, a leopard suddenly leaped out of the forest in front of her.

Yorks paper

Order your nuts NOW. If you have any difficulty, drop me a envelope addressed to yourself and marked 'Nuts'.

Gardening column in *Reveille*

PC Roberts said he found the horse straying riding the bicycle. Noticing he was swaying a good deal, and that he had no trouser clips on, witness stopped him and questioned him about the cycle.

Kent paper

The bride, who was given away by her father, wore a dress of white figured brocade with a trailing veil held in place by a coronet of pearls. She carried a bouquet of rose buds and goods vehicles, leaving free access to all private vehicles not built for more than seven passengers.

Atherstone News and Herald

If you have a sack that is full of holes don't throw it away, empty them out into a clean box and store in the dry; they may be useful when you start bulk planting.

Reading Horticultural Corporation's Garden Topics

If your skin is not liable to be sensitive, rub the arms gently with pumice stone. This will take them right off.

Woman's paper

⊠ DO YOU WANT A PAIR OF GLOVES ⊠
⊠ MADE FROM YOUR OWN SKIN? ⊠

Advert in London weekly

The eminent statistician rubbed his ear thoughtfully and produced a cigarette.

Short story

In reply to your valued inquiry, we enclose illustrations of Dining Tables of Oak, seating fourteen people with round legs and twelve people with square legs, with prices attached.

Huntly Express

WOMAN HURT WHILE COOKING HER HUSBAND'S BREAKFAST IN A HORRIBLE MANNER

Headline in Texas paper

Break the eggs carefully into a basin taking care not to break the eggs.

Cookery book

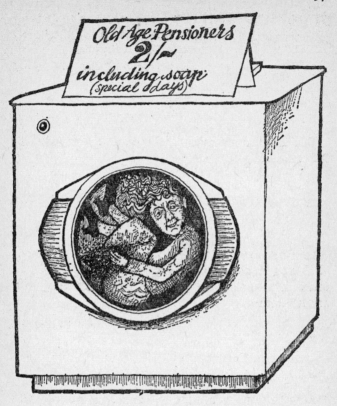

◇ Up to 13 lbs dry weight for
only 2/9 including soap

◇ Blankets 1/9 each including soap

◇ Old Age Pensioners 2/- including soap
(special days).

Leaflet from Laundry and Dry Clean centre

Amid the cheers of their many friends in the farming community the bride and groom cut the wedding cake made by Mrs Luston (shaped like a haystack on stilts).

Dayton, Ohio, paper quoted in *Evening Standard*

The possibility that the gang would try to smuggle the gold to India or Pakistan – where gold is worth three times its value in Britain – led to a special watch at Heathrow Airport and a special check being ordered on any ship sailing there.

Birmingham paper

In a bitterly cold wind, the Queen, wearing a warm sage-green tweed coat with a beaver lamb collar and a green mitre installation of turbo-alternators and boilers.

Essex paper

The committee expressed the view that the school-crossing patrolman could best assist the children if he were dead outside the school entrance.

Public Services

BANGKOK

Sir, For the case that your electric light should fail we beg to send you enclosed a postcard which please send us at once when you find your light out. The Company will then send you another postcard.

Yours truly,

Manager, Siam Electricity Co Ltd

● Dip your soiled face in alcohol, rinse it in the liquid and hang it straight out to dry. It may then be pressed.

Toronto Mail

Dear Sirs,
   My baby was so nervous that it nearly went into spasms at every loud noise. I saw your advertisement and gave it T—— Syrup, and it is all over it.

A testimonial

Because there has been some misunderstanding as to which Mrs Wood has been ill, we wish to tell readers of the Bulletin that it is Mrs Lucille Wood and not Mrs Lucille Wood. There, that will clear that up!

Church bulletin

Mrs Lukes was caught beneath the auto and taken to St Joseph's Hospital with several fractured bones. The bones were on their way to Woonsocket to spend their holiday.

Connecticut paper

One of these men, a Calabrian named Motta, went to his partner's shop and tried to shoot him while he was engaged in shaving a customer. The bullet shaved the face of a boy who was waiting.

Egyptian Gazette

Erwen was a man of keen observation. There was something in his visitor's eyes which puzzled him. Suddenly he realized what it was. It was the whisky and soda which he had set down untasted at the corner of the table.

From a serial by E. Phillips Oppenheim

☆　When the baby is done drinking it must be unscrewed and laid in a cool place under a tap. If the baby does not thrive on fresh milk it should be boiled.

Women's magazine

P. T. Harris gained credit for himself and for Wellingborough Grammar School by passing in every subject and gaining four distinctions – in arithmetic, French, algebra, and Little Bowden Pig Club.

Market Harborough Advertiser

Wrap poison bottles in sandpaper and fasten with scotch tape or a rubber band. If there are children in the house, lock them in a small metal box.

Philadelphia Record

Headaches? Let us examine your eyes and help you in removing same

Notice in optician's window

In the preliminary examination of patients the author introduces a test that is new to us; two or three breaths having been drawn through the nose, this organ is then punched by the anaesthetist, whilst the patient holds his breath as long as possible.

The Practitioner

The seaman, severely injured when the ship was three hours out, was taken to hospital and the hippopotamus removed.

The Daily Telegraph

YOU CAN SKATE MORE THAN ONE MILE ON ONE SLICE OF BREAD

Saturday Evening Post

Judge Julius H. Miner yesterday granted a decree of separate maintenance to a wife who said her husband left her sitting alone in taverns while he danced with chairs and spaghetti.

Chicago Sun-Times

When the express arrived the superintendent of the local zoo was summoned, and after a three hours' struggle he was lassoed and pulled into a waiting case.

Sunday paper

BLANK'S MACARONI AND CHEESE
IN
TOMATO SAUCE

containing

TOMATO SAUCE, MACARONI and CHEESE

Label on tin

Our 'ETERNA' Fountain-pen is a revolting invention.

German pamphlet

We do not tear your clothes with machinery

We do it carefully by hand

Sign in laundry window

Dr Guy Suits, assistant to the director of the General Electric Company research laboratory, has again been named one of the United States.

Schenectady Union Star

The Hon Treasurer (Mr Hodgson) stated that he was willing to carry on in his office until he had to move from the town, which might be at any time (applause).

Andover Advertiser

WANTED Smart Young Man for butcher's. Able to cut, skewer and serve a customer.

Advert in local paper

The millinery department will be on the second floor and the proprietor states that their aim will be to always have the latest and last word in women's hats at appalling prices.

Union City (Indiana) *Times*

! **GREAT SHOE OFFER** !
Every pain guaranteed

Advert in provincial paper

Don't decide now. Have the set in your own home. After two days trial we will call for your derision.

Bedford paper

FOR we regret to state that Mr Armar, who is seriously ill at his residence, showed slight signs of improvement yesterday.

West Indian paper

On Wednesday of last week, two children of William Pass, near New London, fell into a 20-foot well accidentally. Fortunately the well was dry and the youngsters fell on top of one another so that their fall was broken.

Oxford (Pennsylvania) *News*

FOR SALE

A rarely comfortable
modern detached residence

Apply Blank & Co, Dublin

Irish Times

'Heavens, I am thirty!' she said. 'Please get me a drink.'
Magazine story

Mrs Oscar Maddox is able to be up after being confined to bed for several weeks with malaria fever, to the delight of her friends.

Thomasville (Georgia) *Times-Enterprise*

Nurse wanted; one boy aged 14 months, willing to do own nurseries and washing.

Daily paper

The carpet is your children's playground. Have them beaten or shampooed by our improved method.

Tradesman's circular

CHILDREN
FOUND STRAYING
WILL BE TAKEN TO
THE LION HOUSE

Notice in Zoo

DEAR MISS DIX – A certain man has asked me to marry him, and I do not know whether to say 'yes or ETAOIN N N' – Miss Anxious.

Tampa Tribune

Horace picked up a shabby-looking volume. His ear, keen for an approaching footstep, turned over the leaves.

Guernsey paper

The referees must put the ball in the scrums but not necessarily be rolled along the ground.

New Zealand paper

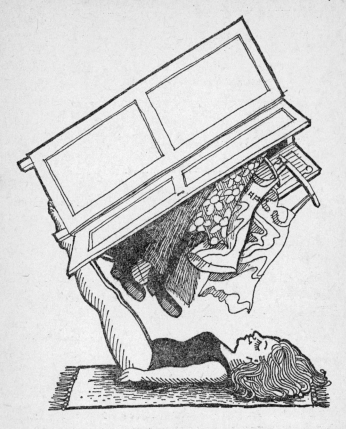

Lie flat on the back, with the feet tucked under the wardrobe. Keep the hands at the sides and raise the legs until they are vertical. Very slowly lower again.

South African paper

WANTED – Man to clean pig's feet; piece-work.

Advert in *Liverpool Echo*

The troupes of monkeys are guaranteed to keep patrons laughing, riding bicycles, and balancing on huge balls.

Hawaiian paper

Dorking police suspect that the recent thefts from cars could be the work of one person or a gang.

Dorking Advertiser

Coo forty-five minutes and cover with a layer of sliced tomatoes. Season lightly with salt and pepper and coo until meat is very tender.

Beverley Hills Shopping News

| GREENLAND VOLCANO IN ERUPTION |
| By arrangement with *The Times* |

The Scotsman

Save time and cut fingers with a parsley mincer.

This Week

The half-starving man sat down at the rough deal table and began to eat it ravenously.

Sunday paper serial

Lady desires post; domesticated, fond of cooking children.

Advert in weekly paper

Drop hot cooked rice into hot soap by spoonfuls and you will have rice dumplings.

Indiana paper

In evidence Mr Jowett said the idea was that he and the defendant should go into partnership with the hens.

Craven Herald and Pioneer

The Women's Society of Christian Service of the Methodist Church entertained the senior girls and teachers of Yale schools with a tea Tuesday afternoon. Guests were revived from 4 PM to 5 PM in the home of Mrs John Dennis.

Cushing (Oklahoma) *Daily Citizen*

It would be a great help towards keeping the churchyard in good order if others would follow the example of those who clip the grass on their own graves.

from a Parish magazine

Opinions differ on what constitutes eating sensible food. In my informant's view it includes eating Crean and his Orchestra.

Notts paper

At a police-controlled crossing drivers who wish to turn right should wait for the All Clear before running over the policeman.

Translated from *Hamburger Nachrichten*

Q. What does the thread count printed on the label of bed sheets and pillowcases indicate?
A. The Massacre of Fort Mickinac in 1763 by Chief Pontiac of the Ottawas.

Columbus (Ohio) *Citizen*

Germans are so small that there may be as many as one billion, seven hundred million of them in a drop of water.

Mobile Press

Revolting Police
take over
Bolivia

Headline in Iowa paper

The window of the schoolroom was too small for him to squeeze through. Keith scratched his head and did some rapid thinning.

Story in boys' paper

The Bishop of Bristol was the sole occupant of the Episcopal Bench. He, having said prayers, stayed for the event of the day. The other Lords just looked in, swore, and went out again.

Irish Times

But gentlemen, I maintain we should turn a deaf ear to any other red herring that may be drawn across our path.

Report of speech

Besides schoolchildren, motorists are often compelled in springtime to include frogs and toads among their objects of compulsory nature study; because you cannot help noticing some of the things which you kill.

Motoring journal

Lady having spent Christmas with her family, strongly recommends comfortable homely hotel.

Advert in Sussex paper

At a demonstration of Colour Television recently, there were shown a man eating a piece of watermelon, a pot of geraniums, and a young woman in a coloured frock.

Essex paper

CORRECTION. An impostor with a morbid sense of humour was responsible for publication in the *Times-Picayune* last Wednesday of a notice announcing the death of Mrs Gloria Lagman. Mrs Lagman is alive. We regret, of course, the necessity for this correction.

New Orleans *Times-Picayune*

A houseowner in Golders Green was forced to leave his house through dangerous cracks in the walls.

Hendon paper

Two-room basement apartment, hot and cold water, shower in basement. Almost private bath.

Advert in *Lawrence* (Kansas) *Journal-World*

Lawrence Beal has recovered from a visit to relatives in Newcastle N. H. and Boston.

Ellsworth (Maine) *American*

Man's Wellington boots, size 8, perfect for cobalt or mauve cock budgie.

Advert in *Exchange and Mart*

One main event in London was Cruft's Dog Show at Olympia. For two days dogs and dog-owners from all over the country crowded the huge halls and galleries, barking at one another in fierce competition.

Aberdeen Press and Journal

HENS IN THE UNITED STATES
LAY 700 EGGS A SECOND

New Zealand paper

> To Sell or Let
> House and Garden, Cow and Horse Stable
> Two Conservatives and
> Useful Garden

Advert in Dorset paper

This article will be a great boon to amateur poultry keepers. It gives the secret of hatching chickens in a nutshell.

Kent paper

> HORSES, PLEASE KEEP THIS GATE SHUT

Notice in Sussex field

The driver having finished milking, his cow offered to take me into an adjoining room, saying that while waiting for the manager I could see where the milk was cooled.

British Medical Journal

He put the melting honey-coloured fruit on her plate and got out a silk handkerchief. She began to eat it thoughtfully.

Serial in provincial paper

He bent swiftly and found her lips and, without removing them from her mouth, lifted her to her feet and drew her into his arms.

from *There is a destiny* by Sonia Deane

We reserve the right to refuse admittance to any child that is too unruly to cause confusion in the school.

Prospectus of Alabama school

Their house was full of little birds and I can see them to this day sitting on the sofa, holding hands and beaming.

Story in women's magazine

School record for 100 yards was broken at Kingswood (Bath) School sports, when three boys, R. K. Brown, J. Harris and Victor Ludorum dead-heated in 10-3/5 seconds.

Evening paper

'Here's Miller running in to bowl. He's got two short legs and one behind.'

BBC commentator

I bet I'm the only bloke who's chased a rabbit on a motor-bike round and round a field *and* caught the rabbit.

Story in *Woman's Own*

In the last two rounds both threw non-stop punches to the acclaim of an enthusiastic audience, but the British boy was hitting the cleaner.

Evening Standard

Complete home for sale. Two dble, one single bed, dining rm, three piece suite, wireless, television, carpets, lion, etc.

Advert in *Portsmouth Evening News*

FOR SALE – A beautiful light chestnut-coloured cold. Owner has had it for two years. Very high-spirited and needs careful handling.

Advert in Berkshire paper

William Sparks, grocer, was fined 40s. for selling bread containing 93.08% of Epsom salts, which a medical officer declared was injurious to health.

Liverpool Echo

WE LOSE $10 ON EVERY SALE BUT WE MAKE IT UP BECAUSE OF OUR ENORMOUS VOLUME

Advert in Philadelphia paper

As this garment is shrink-resisting, rubbing will cause rapid shrinkage, and this fact cannot be over-emphasized.

Label on shirt

The Editor wishes to thank the Rector for his kind help in editing this issue during her absence, and apologizes for its shortcomings on that account.

Parish magazine

'He must have been drunk, because he proposed to a police woman on his way to the station,' said Superintendent Jones.

Stratford-upon-Avon *Herald*

Detectives making last-minute inquiries went to a stable in Berkshire today. They wanted to interview the occupier.

Evening Standard

BURGLAR CRACKS VICTIM'S SKULL
FINDS NOTHING

Headline in American paper

At the Sunday evening service the anthem 'To Thee O Lord our Hearts we Raise' was rendered by the choir. The work of re-roofing the church began on Monday.

Manx paper

To prevent tears when peeling onions, either bite on a slice of bread or work under a running tap and breathe through the mouth.

Daily Express

Puzzles and Games

Piccolo Book Selection

These and other PICCOLO Books are obtainable from all booksellers and newsagents. If you have any difficulty please send purchase price plus 7p postage to P.O. Box 11, Falmouth, Cornwall.

While every effort is made to keep prices low, it is sometimes necessary to increase prices at short notice. PAN Books reserve the right to show new retail prices on covers which may differ from those advertised in the text or elsewhere.